Twice Born

Written & illustrated
By Margie Galliver

**A NEW
LIGHT
EXPERIENCE**

www.newlightexperience.com

This book is dedicated to all the children I have met and to those I have never met. It is easy to see heaven in the faces of children and I have attempted to include a little bit of heaven in this story for them and for those who love them.

Twice Born

from isBooks Parent Participation Bible series
is now available as an Image Sound Book
on DVD or as an Ebook and on Kindle
at
www.newlightexperience.com

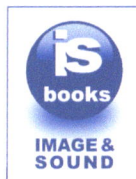

The waters of the Jordan stirred
and shimmered in the sun,

in little gems of darting lights
encircling everyone...

and rippled rings of water
spread outward to the banks,

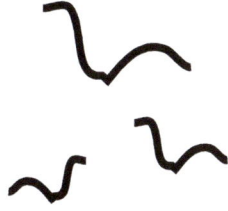

as crowds of people stood in turn
and quietly gave thanks.

They all had come from near and far
the message they had heard,
of such a one whom God had sent
to come and spread the Word.

His name was John the Baptist
a holy man was he,
he used his days to pray and fast
the reason was you see...

that God had spoken to his heart,
John heard His voice one day...

God told John to prepare a path
and straighten out a way...

a way for one so mighty,
so beautiful and kind...

John came to tell the people that
the Saviour they would find...

if they could open up their hearts
be sorry in God's sight,
he'd wash away their sins of old
and bathe them in the light...

a light that shines all day,
all night,
forever without end

and fills all hearts
with peace and joy
until one day they blend...

together in a family
where every son and daughter,
is baptized in the light of love
and born again of water.

The people pondered
in their hearts
the truth could surely be,
that John the Baptist
was the Christ
of ancient prophesy,

but John gave them the answer
he told them publicly,
that such a one was yet to come
more mightier than he.

He comes with fire
that doesn't burn
to baptize you with Spirit,
and fill your heart
with light and grace
and place his love within it.

And there it was that Jesus stood
his gaze fixed up above,
and heaven opened up it's gate...

and then flew down a dove.

It was the Holy Spirit,
descending from on high,
and rested there with Jesus...

the people all stood by...

a voice came down from heaven now,

they heard it and believed...

'This is My Beloved Son,
in whom I am well pleased.'

www.ingramcontent.com/pod-product-compliance
Lightning Source LLC
LaVergne TN
LVHW010024070426

835508LV00001B/39